Dreams and Visions

Written by

Linda Wells

Copyright © 2013 Linda Wells.

All rights reserved. No part of this book may be used or reproduced by any means, graphic, electronic, or mechanical, including photocopying, recording, taping or by any information storage retrieval system without the written permission of the publisher except in the case of brief quotations embodied in critical articles and reviews.

WestBow Press books may be ordered through booksellers or by contacting:

WestBow Press
A Division of Thomas Nelson
1663 Liberty Drive
Bloomington, IN 47403
www.westbowpress.com
1-(866) 928-1240

Because of the dynamic nature of the Internet, any web addresses or links contained in this book may have changed since publication and may no longer be valid. The views expressed in this work are solely those of the author and do not necessarily reflect the views of the publisher, and the publisher hereby disclaims any responsibility for them.

Any people depicted in stock imagery provided by Thinkstock are models, and such images are being used for illustrative purposes only.

Certain stock imagery © Thinkstock.

ISBN: 978-1-4497-9679-2 (sc)
ISBN: 978-1-4497-9678-5 (e)

Library of Congress Control Number: 2013909608

Printed in the United States of America.

WestBow Press rev. date: 6/10/2013

Dreams and Visions ~

sister was seven, I was nine and my older sister was eleven. My mom had her hands full with all of us kids, going to school and working too. She was a very strong willed person. Mom knew what she wanted and she went for it. My mom took all the classes she could handle and finished school a year early. For one and half years our family was apart. Mom had to go to a bigger college to get her degree in teaching school. My little sister and I stayed with mom. My older sister and brother stayed with my dad. We would go home on the weekends. Then on Monday morning early we would go back to where my mom went to college.

My mom still had to work. So she went to work at the library. In the evening my little sister and I would stay at the library until it was time for mom to get off work. I still don't know how mom did all that she did. At night she would stay up late to study. That was when she had quite time. My mom has encouraged me so much in life. If there is something you want in life go for it. If you give it your all, you can reach your goal in life. Mom later got her master degree. She taught at one school for twenty-three years.

My dad had some bad habits. It was drinking, hanging out in the bars and chasing women. It caused a lot of problems in life and we went through a lot of hard times. Dad and mom would have arguments and also fights. I watched mom and dad fight a lot. It is hard to go through things like that in life. Sometimes when dad would come in at night, we knew that he would be drunk and that there would be a fight. I think that some bad habits are really a sickness. You need help to get rid of your bad habits. I loved my dad dearly. I just did not like the way he lived his life. My mom tried to have things in life. But dad would sell a lot of our things, so he could have the money to drink. We came home from school one day and the television was gone. Dad had sold it to have money to drink on. They could have had a lot of things, but it takes two people that want the same thing.

Mom would go to church sometimes. After awhile dad would get mad and she would stop going to church. When I was twelve years old I had went to church one Sunday. I was sitting there listening to the preacher talk about heaven and hell. I was scared and at the end of the service I went up and told the pastor I did not want to go to hell. I wanted to be saved. I got baptized the following Sunday. I did not go to church much after that. My life did not change and I still lived my life as I always did.

When I was nineteen years old I got married. I think sometimes that I got married to get away from all of the fighting. I loved my mom and dad. I just got tired of all the fighting. I married a man that like to drink also. My husband's name is Don. I know you are thinking, why did I marry someone that drank? I was looking for a way out of the fighting that I went through with my mom and dad. I know it doesn't make sense. Sometimes life just doesn't make a lot of sense. I even tried drinking and I just didn't like it. I would feel guilty when I did drink. My father-in-law also drank beer. I would go to the bars with my husband and sat and drink pop. It was either go with him to the bars or sit home by myself. I did not go to church after I got married. We had our share of arguments too.

My mom and dad were separated for a few months, but that was nothing new. They did that off and on in their marriage. Dad came to my house one day with his girlfriend Jane. Dad told me he was going to marry her. Jane had some money and I think that was why my dad was going to marry her. I didn't think much of what he said. I figured dad would go back to mom as always. That day my mom had made an appointment for the whole family to have pictures made. We were going to have our first family portrait taken. Dad and I went to have pictures taken. Jane stayed at my house when we went to get pictures taken. All I could think about was dad's girlfriend was at my house waiting for dad to get back. Every time I look at the family portrait I think about dad's girlfriend being at my house that day. I could not tell my mom. I knew it would hurt her.

A few months later my dad called me. It was on Thanksgiving Day in 1981. Dad knew all the family was having dinner at my house. Everyone had already left and went home. Dad told me he had gotten married and for me to tell mom. That was so hard to do. Mom and dad had separated so many times .I thought that they might get back together. I think mom felt the same way. I knew I had to go and tell mom. So I called my little sister Sue. I told her she was going with me. So the next day we went and told mom. She did not take it very well. Mom still loved dad even though they had their problems. I was around seven months pregnant at the time. My little sister Sue was also pregnant. We were trying to stay calm about the whole situation. I was twenty-one at that time. It was hard to see my mom and dad separate. We did not get to spend holidays together as a family. Mom and dad were married almost twenty-five years. I know they were better off to separate. The marriage was so bad, I was afraid that one of them might really get hurt. Us kids would scream and cry when they were fighting. Some people say they would like to start their life over again, not me. I would not want to go through that again. I think when we go through things like that it makes us stronger and appreciate the good things in life.

After about four months went by, my brother introduced mom to a man that he knew. His name was Tom. I remember the night I went to the hospital to have my baby. Mom and Tom stayed all night when I was in labor. The next morning on March 5, 1982 Paul. was born. Having a baby I thought would change my husband's way of living. I was so wrong about that.

Mom and Tom got married a few months later. Tom was very good to my mom. Whatever she wanted he would do. He did all he could to please mom. He was a good stepdad to us kids. He treated us like we were his own kids. Tom was a person who would joke around and have a good time. If you ever met him, you would not forget him. He would make you laugh anytime you were around him. Tom was always one that would help anyone who needed it. He was just that kind of man. Mom and Tom had a ranch about eight miles out of town. They had cows and horses. They also opened a team roping area. Mom would make chili dogs and hamburgers. Mom was well known for her chili. Some people would come to the roping just to get one of her chili dogs. Mom and Tom had a lot of friends. Mom finally was able to have things in life.

My mom was so happy with Tom. Mom loved to play music. She could play about any instrument that you put in her hand. I saw Tom load mom's instruments up so many times and take her to play music. They shared so many good times together. Mom had finally found a man that would do things with her. God blessed mom with that marriage.

Dreams and Visions ~

My dad was married for about sixteen years. Then his wife Jane passed away. Later he got married again to a woman named Carol. They were only married just about three years and then they got divorced. Dad still lived his life the way he wanted. Went to the bars and drank his beer. At the end of his life he was alone. Dad had never stopped loving mom. They just couldn't live together. They cared for each other. Sometimes a house isn't big enough to share with another person, when you have so many different interests in life. It is so sad that such bad habits can hurt so many people in life.

As the years went by my husband still drank his beer. It caused us a lot of problems. Don was a good provider and a hard worker. On his days off was his time to do what he wanted. That was to set around and drink beer or go to the bars. We never had friends to do things with. Don would not take me out to dinner. I always had to go and pick up our food and bring it home. He never did things with me or our son. I would try and get him to do things with our son, but it never happened. Our son never got to spend quality time with his dad.

When my son Paul started kindergarten I started

cleaning houses. My husband did not want me to work. I told him I would clean houses while our son was at school and he agreed. I started cleaning house for an elderly couple. Their names were Kim and John. They were a very sweet couple. I had worked for them for awhile when John invited me to go to church with him. Kim was on a walker and did not get around to good, so she would watch preaching on the television. I never went to church with John. He found out he had cancer in his throat. John started taking treatments. Months went by and he was not getting any better.

I started cleaning house for about four other people too. I was sitting at the house one day thinking of all the people I cleaned for. I thought they are all Christians. The Lord was working on me then and I didn't even notice it until later. The Lord does so much for us that we don't even notice.

My mother-in-law and I were very close. We would talk every day and I would see her two or three times a week. We lived in the same town. One day we found out that she had cancer too. After test was done the doctors recommend that she take treatments too. My mother-in-law's name was

Tammy. My husband worked, so I started taking my mother-in-law for her treatments five days a week. I had to drive about fourty-five miles one way. Tammy started church and it didn't take long for me to start going to church. I went to church every Sunday with my mother-in-law. The more I listened to the pastor I knew that I needed to rededicate my life to the Lord. It had been a long time since I had went to church. I held on to the back of the church pews for months. Then one day I let go of the church pew and went up and rededicated my life to the Lord. I became a member of the church. Later we found out that the cancer had spread into five different parts of Tammy's body. The doctors gave her around six months to live. I remember her standing up in church when she could barely walk. I would tell her it was ok to sit. She would stand up every time. She was so weak that I would help her up. She loved the Lord so much. She was the sweetest person I know. She always said "if you can't say something nice, don't say anything at all."

One day I was at Kim and John's cleaning house and his wife told me that they were taking him to the doctor. Kim had talked to the doctor and the doctor said there was no more they could do for him. Before they left and went to the doctor John had a friend there visiting him. John took me by the arm and told his friend "I am praying for this girl." I thought he is praying for me. This man is dying and yet he was praying for me. It touched me so much.

About a week had passed by and the phone rang and I answered it. It was his wife Kim. She said "honey have you forgot about us?" I said "oh no, I have not forgotten about you and John." That was all I was thinking about. I was running away because I was scared and did not know what to do. After Kim called me I knew I had to work up the courage to go and see them. It took me a couple of days and I went over to see them. John was in a coma and could not talk. I stayed and visited with his wife and son for around an hour. They were staying up around the clock with him. I knew John's sister, her name is Helen. I cleaned her house too. I went home and told my husband I wanted to set up with Helen one night. My husband told me I had too much to do. I was taking my mother-in-law for treatments. My son was twelve years old and I would always be home before he got in from school. I think my husband thought I had enough to do. He did not want me to take on more than I could handle. He was so thankful for me taking his mom to her treatments.

Something kept telling me to go and see John that Friday. I told my husband I was going over there Friday. I went over to see them. John's brother-in-law was there and John's son Jeff. Kim his wife was sitting on the couch. Jeff told me his mom had not had lunch. Jeff asked me if I would try and get her to eat something. Jeff left and went home. After about ten or fifteen minutes I took Kim into the kitchen and fixed her a sandwich. She had eaten about half of the sandwich when her brother came into the kitchen and said. "Kim you need to come in here." She got up as fast as she could and went into the living room where her husband laid in a hospital bed. Kim saw him take his last breathe and so did I. It was the first time I saw someone die. I was devastated. I went outside and sat on a bench. I just needed to be alone for awhile. I left after about twenty minutes.

I went to where my husband worked and told him what had happened. I knew I had to go and tell my mother-in-law. It was so hard to do. I knew she did not have too much longer herself. She was setting on the bed in the bedroom. When I told her she looked down at the floor and did not say much.

I was going to church every week. It had been six months that I was in church. I was hearing God's word. How Jesus took my place on the cross and died for my sins. I realized I was not saved when I was twelve years old. God knows what it would take for me to come to him. It was seeing someone take their last breathe. God used John to the very end of his life leading me to the Lord. It is sad that sometimes it takes such tremendous things in life for us to go to the Lord.

The next day after John passed away, I was sitting at my kitchen table by myself. I asked God into my life and said "I need you Lord." It was then that I truly got saved. My life changed so much. I realized that Jesus took my place on the cross for my sins. I knew that I was a sinner and I asked God to forgive me of my sins. It was then I realized how much love the Lord had for me. John chapter 3 verse 16; For God so loved the world that he gave his only begotten Son, that whosoever believeth in him should not perish, but have everlasting life.

I wanted to know more of God's word. I kept

Dreams and Visions ~

thinking how John was praying for me. God puts people into your life for a reason. John passed away in August of 1995. My mother-in-law Tammy passed away in October of 1995. Just two months later. I keep going to church after I lost my mother-in-law. There were times my husband did not want me to go to church. I told him I was going. We would have words and then I would go to church. I remember crying on my way to church a lot of times. My heart was so broken. I needed God in my life to handle all these things. I knew I could not do this by myself.

My father-in-law had been sick before my mother-in-law passed away. A few months went by and we finally got my father-in-law to go to the doctor. You could have knocked us over with a feather. We found out that he had cancer too. The doctors gave my father-in-law about six months to live. I was reading the bible a lot and wanting to know more about Jesus. I needed the Lord to help me through all the things I was going through. My father-in-law was going for treatments to. My sister-in-law and I were taking turns taking him for radiation five days a week. His name was Joe. One day he got sick and was admitted to the hospital. I knew then I could not take him any longer for his treatments. My husband started taking his dad for treatments. It was meant to be. For my husband got to spend more time with his dad.

One day I was setting at the house and was thinking about Joe. Did he know the Lord as his savior? I did not know if he did or not. I could not get it off my mind. It is hard to witness to family members. Something kept telling me to go and talk to him about the Lord. So I went and talked to him and asked him if he knew the Lord as his savior. Joe told me he did. It is hard to lose a loved one. If you know they are saved and going to spend eternity in heaven with the Lord, it is such a comfort to you. We all will leave this world someday and spend eternity in heaven or hell.

One night I was setting in my recliner, reading the bible in Revelations chapter one verses thirteen through seventeen. And in the midst of the seven candlesticks one like unto the Son of man, clothed with a garment down to His head and foot, and girt about the paps with a golden girdle. His head and his hairs were white like wool, as white as snow; and his eyes were as a flame of fire; and his feet like

Dreams and Visions ~

unto fine brass, as if they burned in a furnace; and his voice as the sound of many waters. And he had in his right hand seven stars; and out of his mouth went a sharp two-edge sword; and his countenance was as the sun shineth in his strength. And when I saw him, I fell at his feet as dead. And he laid his right hand upon me, saying unto me, Fear not; I am the first and the last.

I went to bed that night and had a dream. This is my dream. Out of nowhere I saw a bright whirlwind just spinning. I was afraid. I remember thinking, where did this come from? Right then I heard a soft and gentle voice telling me "don't be afraid. I am Jesus." Then I looked up and I saw such a very bright ray of light and I saw a white robe and a outline of Jesus. I looked again to see his face, but I could not see his face. The light was so bright I could only look for a very short time. I could feel such a peace no words can describe what I felt. It is a peace we will never feel here on earth. I know one day I will feel it again. It will be when I stand in the presence of the Lord. For the third time I looked up to see his face. I could see everything but his face. Then I bowed so gracefully to the Lord. I remember feeling so unworthy to be in the presence of the Lord. I did not want to leave his presence. When I looked up Jesus was gone. I was so disappointed. I wanted to stay in the Lord's presence. It was such the most wonderful feeling you could ever have. I was ready to spend eternity with the Lord. I was so thankful for what the Lord had showed me. Then I said "Lord do not let me forget this dream." For I knew I was having a dream. I did not wake up until that morning. I slept so peacefully through the night. When I just started to wake up, I had not even opened my eyes. I started remembering my dream. I started crying. I just stayed in bed for awhile. Thinking about the dream I had just had. I remembered every detail. After a little while, I got up out of bed and went to tell my husband. I could not even talk for crying. I told him the dream and I think my husband thought I was crazy. He did not believe me. I had my dream June 22, 1996. I kept thinking about my dream. I could not get it off my mind. I thought Lord, why did I receive such a wonderful blessing from you. That day I told my sister-in-law about my dream.

    A few days before that something kept telling me to call Joe's brother Phil. He lived in Alabama. So

I picked up the phone and told Phil that his brother was not feeling well. Phil and his wife came down the next day. They lived about ten hours away.

We did not like my father-in-law living by himself. He would not stay with us and he would not let us stay with him. We were afraid something would happen to him and he would be there by himself. Phil and his wife stayed with Joe when they came down. My husband and I would always call my father-in-law everyday. We would check on him and see if he needed anything. Sometimes five or six times a day. We went over to see my husband's uncle and aunt. We visited with them for just a little while. They needed to rest from the trip. On the second day they were there, we spent half the day at Joe's house. My husband and I went home that evening. We just lived about ten blocks away. It was around five p.m. that evening. We took our baths and watched a little television. We went to bed around 10:00 p.m. We had not been a sleep very long and the phone rang. It was Phil on the phone. He told us to hurry up and get over there. By the time we got there, Joe had already passed away. Joe passed away on June twenty-fourth 1996. Two days after I had my dream.

Later I realized that God had used me to call his brother and to tell him to come down. My father-in-law did not pass away there by himself. The Lord has everything planned out for all of us. We might not understand it until later. I am so thankful God is in charge. When we make plans the Lord must look upon us and chuckle. All things are in God's hands. Remember we had just lost my mother-in-law eight months and twelve days before that.

After my father-in-law passed away, my husband did not morn like he should have. He just got very upset and mad. I told him to cry and it would help, but he just stayed mad. He was very short with me. Months went by and our marriage was getting worse. I then realized my dream was to help me to get through this. I would remember my dream and the peace I felt. I knew the Lord was with me and helping me each day. It took about a year for things to get better. My husband's heart was so broken and he had been through so much. Losing his parents so close together was really hard for him.

I asked the Lord, why did I receive the dream?

Dreams and Visions ~

I am not worthy to be so blessed. I kept asking the Lord over and over. I started reading the bible even more. I wanted to know more about Jesus. I was reading in Exodus chapter 33 verses 20and 23 and I read this. Thou canst not see my face; for thou shall no man see me, and live. And I will take away mine hand, and thou shalt see my back parts; but my face shall not be seen. I then realized why I could not see his face. No one will see his face until it is time for us to be with him. I told a few people about my dream. Mostly family and friends I would tell. Each time I would tell my dream, it made me feel like I just had the dream. It refreshed me so much. I loved telling it even though I have had all kinds of looks from people. I knew that some of them did not believe.

My heart was so burdened for my family, because none of them went to church. A few years later my mother and step dad started church. My brother also started to church. When the Lord would lay it on my heart to talk to people about the Lord I would. I gave my two sisters a bible and talked to them about the Lord. There were times when I would go and see my dad and I would talk to him about the Lord. I would read scriptures to him. My dad never learned to read or write. My grandpa would read the bible to them when they were younger. My dad knew more about the bible than I thought. Dad said "I have done too many bad things in life for the Lord to forgive me." I said "dad if you asked from your heart and really mean it. Admit you are a sinner and realize that Jesus died on the cross for your sins. God will forgive you of anything you have done." I felt like I was not getting through to dad. But each time the Lord would lead me to talk to dad I did.

I was still going to church by myself. I knew I needed to get baptized. I did not want to admit that I was not saved before. It took me over four years before I would get baptized. One night I was in bed and I could not go to sleep. I had been at a church social for the pastor that night. The pastor was leaving our church. I stayed in bed for awhile thinking about getting baptized. I could not get it off my mind. I did not want to go in front of the church members and tell them I was not saved when I joined the church. I finally said "Lord if I can go to sleep and if I still have that feeling when I go to church, I will walk straight to the pastor and tell him." I went straight to sleep that night. When I

Dreams and Visions ~

woke up that morning I knew what I was going to do. When I entered the church I went straight to the pastor and said "I want to get baptized tonight." It was the pastors last night there. He said "the water might be cold. It might not have enough time to heat up." I said "I do not care." The pastor asked me to stand in front of the members of the church. Tell them that I thought I was saved at twelve years old, but I wasn't. I told them I was truly saved now and that I wanted to get baptized. I worried about what people thought. That is why it took me about four years before I got baptized. We will all stand before the Lord one day and answer to the Lord and no one else. I wonder how many people hold back to give their life to Jesus. Because they are afraid of what people think. Just remember the Lord knows your heart. We are all sinners saved by grace. Romans chapter 3 verse 10. As it is written, There is none righteous, no not one: I had finally gotten baptized and I felt so much better about myself and my relationship with the Lord. That day was May twenty-third 1999.

It is hard living a Christian life, when you are the only one going to church in your family. You can't

~ Linda Wells

share all your feeling with them about the Lord. I would feel so alone at times. I would talk to the Lord so much. I couldn't talk to my husband about the Lord. We were both living our life so different from each other. I was leaning on the Lord and he was drinking his beer.

Our son Paul started drinking when he was thirteen years old. I didn't know it at that time. That was what he was raised up around. I don't know if that was why he started drinking or not. I know it is a very young age to start drinking. When Paul was nineteen he started going with a girl. Her name was Cindy. They went together for around a year and a half. They decided to get married. They bought a trailer house and moved it in our yard. His wife was only sixteen years old. They were both young to get married. My son, Paul was drinking and going to the bars. He would leave his wife at home by herself. Their marriage only lasted about two years. My son was not dealing with his divorce very well. He was staying drunk and going to the bars a lot. Having one child you give them all of your attention. You want the best for your child. My son was not living for the Lord. He was living in such a worldly way.

Dreams and Visions ~

I would pray for him and his safety. I said "Lord I can't watch him all the time, but you can. Lord, watch over him and protect him." I worried about my son so much. A few years went by and things had not changed with my son.

I worked at a grocery store. I found myself praying every morning on my way to work. I would say "Lord how long until my husband and son come to you? When will they give their life to you? When will they start going to church?" I found myself praying more than I ever had. I was constantly praying to the Lord. I must have prayed for about three months. I just needed a sign from the Lord.

One Saturday morning I was on my way to see my mom. She lived about thirty-five miles from my house. It was around eight o'clock in the morning on November twenty-seventh in 2004. I was driving down the road and I was praying for my son. I was getting ready to go around a curve and I saw a white horse standing in the road at an intersection. The horse was facing the east. I slowly put my brakes on. I stopped about thirty feet from the horse. I honked my horn at the horse and it did not move. I waited a few seconds and I honked the horn again, but the horse just stood still. I waited for a few more seconds and for the third time, I honk the horn again. Then I stared at the horse and notice the horse was so still. It did not move at all, or even look at me. The horse was as still as still could be. I stared at the horse for I don't know how long. I think I went into a trance. I just started thinking this is different. I started feeling this is from the Lord. After a little while the horse turned and started walking toward me. The horse walked as though it was walking on clouds. So soft and gentle each step it took. I was startled at first for the horse had been so still. The horse walked right by my car. I could have stuck my hand out the window and touched it. I felt the presence of the Lord so strong. I knew if I could see Jesus, he was setting on the horse. As the horse walked by the car I heard a voice say, "You have seen what I wanted you to see. Don't look back." I never looked back. I set there for a minute and then started driving down the road. It was as though the Lord stopped the world for me. No cars came by at that time. It is a paved country road. I pass cars quite often on that road. There was a house to the left side of the road. I can't tell you how long I sat there. I remembered the

Dreams and Visions ~

scripture in Psalms 46 verse 10. Be still and know that I am God. I kept thinking about what had just happened. I could not get it off my mind. I got to my mom's house and as soon as I walked in the house. I started telling my mom and my aunt about it. My aunt said "You have just been blessed from the Lord." We did not talk about it after that. I stayed for a few hours and visited.

I started home and I could not stop thinking about the white horse. I knew the Lord was telling me something, but I did not know what. All day long that was all I could think about. When I got home I told my husband what happened and he just looked at me as though I had lost it. It seemed like a long day. I was trying to put it all together. That evening I went in to take a shower. It was around eight o'clock. I started thinking about horses and realized there was something about horses in the bible. I thought it is in Revelations. I finished my bath and went into the kitchen where my bible was. I sat down in the chair at the table. My husband was setting in a chair at the table too. I reached and got my bible. As I went to open my bible, it fell open to the exact page the Lord wanted me to read. I looked down to read it and all I could see was the words white horse. I just started crying. I sat there for a minute before I could start reading it. It was in Revelations chapter 19 verses 11-13. **And I saw heaven open, and behold a white horse; and he that sat upon him was called Faithful and True, and in righteousness he doth judge and make war.** His eyes were as a flame of fire, and on his head were many crowns; and he had a name written, that no man knew, but he himself. And he was clothed with a vesture dipped in blood: and his name is called the Word of God.

It was twelve hours from the time I saw the white horse. I had asked the Lord to show me something. I thought it would be a streak of light in the sky or a cloud shaped a certain way. I had been praying a lot for God to show me something. I needed something to help me with my son and husband. I wanted so much for them to start living their life for the Lord and start going to church with me. The Lord was letting me know that he was right there with me. Giving me the comfort I needed so badly at that time in my life. I didn't know how to help my son. The Lord carries us more than we realize. It is one thing to have a dream, but to have a vision too. I was so

Dreams and Visions ~

blessed. I didn't know what to do. I started asking the Lord. "What do you want me to do? You have given me this dream and vision." One day I was looking in the mirror and putting on my make-up. I said "Lord what do I do?" I heard a voice so softly say "tell the people." I said "Lord they will not believe me." The Lord so plainly said "did they believe who I was, when they crucified me on the cross?" I said "oh no Lord or they would not have done it."

It did not take me long to start telling people. I can't tell you how many people I have told. I know there are people that don't believe. I am doing what the Lord wants me to do and that is what matters. I will answer to the Lord one day for the things I have done. How could I not tell people about the dream and vision. The Lord had shown me so much. The more I tell my dream and vision, the more it seems like it was not that long ago. I remember that the Lord is always with me and brings me such peace. I would tell people about my vision. They would ask, where did the white horse go? I told them it did not matter to me. For the Lord showed me, what he wanted me to see.

As time went by, I was reading the bible one day and

in Acts chapter 2 verses 17 and 18 it says. And it shall come to pass in the last days, saith God , I will pour out my spirit upon all flesh: and your sons and daughters shall prophesy, and your young men shall see visions, and your old men shall dream dreams: And on my servants and on my handmaidens I will pour out in those days of my Spirit; and they shall prophesy;

My dad came to my house one day to visit me. We were sitting outside and I started telling him about my vision I had. Dad looked down at the ground as I was telling him. When I finished telling him, he looked up at me and said. "I have heard of people having things like that." I knew right then that my dad believed me. I started praying for my dad so much. At night I would pray. Lord let my dad be saved before he takes his last breathe. I found myself praying this every night when I went to bed. I must have prayed this for months. My dad was not married and living by himself. He was all alone.

One day my dad got sick and was put in the hospital. I would go and see him a few times a week. After dad was in the hospital for a week, he asked to see a pastor. When the pastor got there I told him dad said the Lord will not forgive me. I have done so many bad things in my life. My two sisters, brother and I stayed outside, until the pastor was finished talking to dad. When the pastor came back outside, he gave me the thumbs up. And said "your dad receive Jesus as his savior." Tears started rolling down my face. I had prayed for this so much. When I saw dad I didn't talk about him receiving Jesus as his savior. I thought if he wanted to talk about it he would tell me. Then he told me about an hour later. Dad said "God forgave me of my sins." I said "God forgives us of our sins. It is hard for us to forgive ourselves." Dad looked so strange at me and told me. "That is exactly what the pastor said." See how the Lord works together all things. Romans chapter 8 verse 28: And we know that all things work together for good to them that love God, to them who are the called according to his purpose.

My dad was not getting any better. I went up to the hospital one day and spent the night. I was trying to sleep in a recliner that night beside dad's bed. It was around 4:00 a.m. in the morning and dad started telling me that something was wrong. He said "the room is not the right size. It is like a long hallway." He kept saying it over and over. He started

~ Linda Wells

saying "oh God oh Lord." I said "dad you are saying the right thing." Then dad told me to get the nurse. So I went and got the nurse. The nurse had taken his blood pressure. They checked him out and could not find anything wrong. The nurse said everything was normal. I touched dad's hospital gown and it was very wet. I told dad "everything would be all right." After around two or three minutes dad said "everything is looking normal again." I did not go back to sleep that night. That morning I went home and could not stop thinking about dad. The experience dad had. A few days went by and I went back to the hospital and stayed most of the day. It was February 27, 2007 my dad's birthday. It was his 73rd birthday. We were talking and dad said "Linda I will not live to see another birthday." I could not look at him right then. I turned my back to him, so he could not see my tears rolling down my face. I said "only God knows when our time is up here on earth." Dad knew he was going to leave this world before long. I don't know everything my dad saw that night in the hospital. I think the Lord was preparing dad for his journey home.

The numbers 68 and 73 were in my mind so

much. I thought why do I keep thinking about these numbers? I can't tell you how many times I would think of the numbers. Five days later my dad went to be with the Lord on my mom's 68th birthday. Those two numbers were here. Dad had turned 73 five days early and mom turned 68 the day my dad went to be with the Lord. God had answered my prayer and dad was in the presence of the Lord. Dad was in so much pain. I prayed and said "Lord my dad is ready to be with you. He has accepted you as his savior. Just take him home and not let him hurt anymore." We are never ready to lose a loved one. If you know they are in heaven spending eternity with the Lord it gives you such a comfort. I figure dad just beat me home.

The day of dad's funeral I looked over at my mom and tears was rolling down her cheeks. I had to be strong for my mom. I knew right then that mom still cared for dad. I sat there and remembered how God had put me there to help lead my dad to the Lord. We have memories to hang on too. Dad and I didn't spend a lot of time together. We did not have a lot in common. I lived for the Lord and my dad drank his beer. I could tell dad did not feel comfortable drinking around me. Dad's ex-wife Carol told me that dad said I had a lot of sense. My dad was watching me as I lived my life. We don't think people are watching us that much, but they are. I would have liked to have spent more time with my dad, but it was worth it all to see my dad spend eternity in heaven with our heavenly father.

About a week after dad went to be with the Lord. I was in bed one night and started praying for my dad. Then I said "dad I don't have to pray for you anymore. You are standing in the presence of Jesus and looking upon his face. Feeling such peace no words can describe."

When I would talk to dad about the Lord I felt like I was getting nowhere. The Lord is always working in people's life. Sometimes it may take awhile before we see people start walking the path to the Lord. When they do get there, it is worth the wait. I am so glad I listened to the Lord and talked to my dad. The Lord was leading me all the way. One of my favorite scripture is Philippians 4 verse 13. I can do all things through Christ which strengthens me. If we are only willing to take a step, the Lord will carry us the rest of the way. God will give us the right words to say at the right time. And things will happen in God's time, not ours. People do watch us as we serve God. Just trust in the Lord and let him guide you in life.

Each time I go to see my mom, as I travel down the road. I pass by the place where I had my vision. The white horse and the peacefulness I felt that day. I know the Lord is always with me. And will help me with whatever I may face in my life. I am so thankful that my mom and I could share a relationship with the Lord. As we lose our loved ones it makes us cherish the time we have with them. Tell them the things you want to say now. We might not have a chance to tell them later. Only God knows what tomorrow holds.

My son Paul got married again about five years after his first marriage. I was glad for him. Paul had been so unhappy being by himself. His wife Kate loved him so much. She had a little girl named Nancy from her previous marriage. Nancy was three years old when they got married. They lived in the trailer next door to us. We fell in love with Nancy. She was like our own grandchild. A few years went by and they had a child. They gave us our first grandchild. On March 14, 2010 Amanda was born. She filled our life with so much joy.

It wasn't long after that and things started changing for Paul and his marriage. Paul started going to the bars a lot. The marriage was not going well. They had a lot of arguments. Paul was doing the same thing in this marriage. Living his life the way he wanted too.

In 2010 my step dad went to be with the Lord. He died of cancer too. It is hard to tell a loved one bye. I went to the nursing home and saw Tom. I leaned down over Tom and said "you have been a great step dad to us kids. Tom it is ok to go and be with the Lord. Jesus is waiting with his arms open." I told mom to tell him bye. I think when we tell them bye, it helps them to go on to be with the Lord. Later mom told me that she told Tom bye. Tom went to be with the Lord the next day. My mom lived out in the country. She stayed by herself. We worried about her so much. She was going so much. I told her she was wearing herself out. She said "Linda, if I stay home I think too much." I knew she was thinking about Tom. So mom would go a lot and would not stay home much.

Paul's marriage was getting worse and his

Dreams and Visions ~

wife left him. It broke our hearts. We had our first grandchild. Amanda was almost a year old. We were so upset with the way things were going. Our son was drinking a lot. Going to the bars and leaving his family at home.

One day Paul and a couple of friends went to a bar. His friend Randy was driving a truck that he had just bought. They were gone for a few hours. The phone rang and I answered it. It was Paul. He said "mom I have been in a wreck. I am ok. I am not hurt." I thought what if he is. He had been drinking. I was scared. I told my husband and we called his ex-wife Kate. She came and got us and drove us to where the wreck was. All the way there I prayed Lord let him be ok. When we drove up, I saw our son sitting on the side of the road. I went up to him and I saw blood on his clothes. He told me it was his friend Randy's blood. I said "are you sure you are ok?" He said "yes, mom I am ok." His friend Randy and another guy were already taken by ambulance to the hospital. We drove to the hospital where his friend was. They were getting ready to life flight him to a bigger hospital. Randy was in very bad condition. The other friend had a few cuts and was going to be released that night. That was the first time Paul met the other guy. I don't even know his name.

We went home and Paul was so worried about Randy. We did not sleep much that night. I told our son, let's pray for Randy and we did. Paul told me that Randy had stopped breathing. A man came up to him and asked if there was something he could do. My son said "pray for my brother." He has stopped breathing." When the man took off his hat, Paul recognized him. He was a preacher that Paul knew. When the preacher started praying Randy started breathing. Paul had known Randy since they were about five years old. So Paul called Randy his brother. Paul was twenty-nine at this time in his life. The next morning Paul went up to see him at the hospital. Randy was not doing well. He had a couple of surgeries that night. He was in the hospital for about five or six weeks.

I thought how God had protected our son. It was by God's mercy and grace that Paul did not get hurt. I was praying for the Lord to keep his protective hand on him and the Lord did. Paul said "mom, I should have been hurt." Paul could not understand how he came out of that wreck without a scratch.

I said "the Lord had his arms around you in that wreck."

We found out that our son was on drugs. As time went by Paul was looking so bad. He had lost so much weight. He must have lost thirty pounds or more. He was so skinny. I prayed that God's will be done in my son's life. God knows what is best in each and every situation in life. Sometimes what we may want in life may not be the right thing. Isaiah chapter 55 verse 8: "For my thoughts are not your thoughts, neither are your ways my ways, saith the Lord." I pray that one day my son will have a close relationship with the Lord. I have to remember that God does things at his time. All I can do is pray for my son and hand him over to the Lord. Prayer is a powerful thing. I pray that he will realize how much he needs the Lord in his life. It is hard to let go of your kids. Sometimes that is all we can do. They have to live and learn. You just want the best for your kids. I love my son so much. It hurts when you see them going through so much in life. Sometimes they have to hit rock bottom before they look up. I pray for his safety.

One day when I was at work, a woman that I

got to know, came up and talked to me. She was one of our regular customers. She is a Christian. I started telling her about some of the things I was going through. She took me by the arm and started praying for me. Then she all of a sudden started praying in tongue. I looked up and in my thoughts I said "Lord if you are trying to tell me something I don't understand." At that moment the Lord spoke and said "I have been with you up until now and I will be with you always. I have put you where you are at in life to make you strong." The Lord used that woman to speak to me and remind me that he is there with me all the time. The Lord answered a question that I would ask him so many times. I would say "Lord, why is my life the way it is? Why am I feeling so alone in life? Why do I have to go through these things in life?" I needed to be reminded that the Lord is with me. Whatever I go through here in this world, I know the Lord is with me and is making me strong. The Lord is holding me up and carrying me through this life.

In October 2011 my mom fell on her porch and broke her leg. She had a lady friend coming to get her to take her to the doctor. That is when she found mom laying on her porch. She called a ambulance to come and get her. She had to have surgery. Mom could not get around very good at all. Mom went to a nursing home for about two months. Mom couldn't wait to go home. She wanted to have Christmas at her house, like we always did. Mom went home the middle of December.

We had Christmas at mom's house that year. I had a feeling that would be our last Christmas at mom's house. Mom was not looking very good and seemed to be getting worse. Mom felt so bad on Christmas day that she stayed in her gown and housecoat. That was not like mom. She always dressed up for Christmas. I took pictures that Christmas day knowing it would be our last Christmas with mom. Mom knew that we did not like her living by herself. I know mom would not always tell us how she felt. She did not want us to worry.

I went to mom's house one day and visited with her. When I left that day it broke my heart. I knew mom was getting worse. A few days later she had to go to the hospital. Mom was only in the hospital for a few days when they told us she had too many things wrong with her. They told us kids there was nothing they could do. She only had a few days. We stay at the hospital with her. We called her sisters and brother and told them. The next day they came and saw her. My aunt Betty and I were standing at the side of her bed. All at once I said "Betty lets sing mom a song. She said "what do you want to sing." I said "I don't care. I just want to sing." So Betty said "Amazing Grace." So we started singing. I know my voice was quivering. It was as though God told me to sing. I felt helpless. My mom went to be with the Lord in February 4. 2012.

Paul was still on drugs. I told him I did not want him to come to my mom's funeral. I did not want anyone to see him. He looked so bad. It was hard losing mom and going through everything with Paul. I thought there is nothing I can do for mom now. My son was so young and had so much life ahead of him. I just kept praying.

It has been five years since I lost my dad. I cherished the time I spent with my mom. My mom always had a lot of health problems. I thought she would be the first to go and be with the Lord. Only the Lord knows when our time is up here on earth. I know with all my heart that I will get to see my parents again someday. They are in heaven with the Lord. I miss them both so much. The tears I cry are for me. It is a healing process we go through. I thank the Lord that as the days go by it does get easier for us. We will always have memories and always miss them.

Paul had a great job just a few miles from the house. He lost his job. He had profit sharing and stocks there. A few months after he lost his job they gave him his money. That money almost killed my son. He had money to buy all the drugs he wanted. When you have money, you have a lot of friends. It only took him about six months to go through all that money. His so called friends helped him spend it.

I had a very hard and long year in 2012. My son was so lost. I would watch him fall farther and farther in life. It hurt me and my husband so much. My son still lived in the trailer next door. There was nothing I could do but pray. I talked to God so much. We felt so uncomfortable in our yard. There was so many bad people coming in our yard and jumping the fence and going to Paul's house. I felt like I was living a nightmare. I would always pray "Lord keep your protective hand on my son and keep him safe through all of this."

We felt so much evil spirits on our property and in my son's house. I was over visiting a friend and told her about the evil spirits. Her name is Janet. She is Pentecostal. She asked me if her and her daughters Mary and Jenny could come out and anoint his house. I said "let me ask my son and see if it would be ok." Janet told me she had some oil that was prayed over. She said "would you like to take it home and anoint your house." My husband was so upset and angry about all that our son was doing. I told her yes. I took the oil home. My husband went to the store one day and I was there by myself. I started anointing our house. I knew he would not let me do it when he was there. I had never done this before. I just keep saying "Lord, let your love be felt so strong in this house and be a peaceable home." I put the oil over every widow, chairs, beds and doorway. A few days later Janet and her two daughters Mary and Jenny came out to anoint our son's house. As we started walking over to his house, I asked if they wanted to pray before we went into Paul's trailer. Jenny stopped and said "I was just thinking about that." So we stop and prayed. You could feel such evil spirits. Jenny put oil on Paul and anointed him first. Mary started praying in tongues. After that Jenny interpreted it. God said "I have so many great things ahead for you my son and I love you." I just started crying. They started anointing his house. I wanted to help. I said "Lord I can't pray in tongue, but I am doing the best I can." I ask the Lord "why can't I pray in tongue?" We prayed and anointed the house, property and Paul's truck. It took us around an hour and a half. They stayed around and visited for about thirty minutes. After they left I went in the house and was on my computer. About thirty minutes went by and my husband asked if there was anyone in my family that prayed in tongues. I said "I am not sure if anyone in my family does. I think my aunt might." Just a few minutes later, I looked out the window and saw a person in the driveway. My son said "she was one of the evil ones." My husband went outside to tell her to leave. I sat there and started praying so much. I said "Lord let her feel so uncomfortable on our property. Let her feel your presence so strong." Then all of a sudden I started praying in tongues. That was my first time of praying in tongue. It just starts and takes over. You have no control over it. After the woman left our driveway my husband came in the house. He stopped and stared at me for a moment and walked off. I was still praying in tongue. You can't stop it until it stops. I was thankful, yet I was trying to understand what had just happened. My husband didn't know what to think. I knew right then that I was going to go to Pentecostal Church. I went outside and set down and was trying to grasp what had just happened. It took me a while to realize what had just happened. I was so excited about it. I started calling my friends that had just left my house. I couldn't wait to tell them. When I told them they were so happy for me. They started explaining it to me. They told me it is a gift from God and not everyone receives it. I went to bed that night and started praying in tongue silently. Then it stopped. It wasn't a few minutes later it started again. I got up out of the bed and went into the living room and set on the sofa. I was willing to stay up all night, if that was what the Lord wanted me to do. It lasted about five minutes. Then it stopped.

As days went by I experienced more things. My

Dreams and Visions ~

husband left and went to the store one day. I was cleaning the house and started singing, but I could not understand what I was singing. I thought what am I doing? I picked up the phone and called my friend Janet. I told her what happened and she said "you were singing in tongue." God was giving me so many gifts.

Paul wrecked his truck one day. He ran into an electric pole and smashed the front of the truck in. God was with him again. He didn't get a scratch on him. I was still praying for God to keep his protective hand on our son. I said "God I can't watch over him all the time, but I know you can." I know with all my heart God has a calling for my son. My son will one day get where the Lord wants him to be. He will serve God so much. God has watched over him so much. Paul will tell you he should have died a few times. Paul would go to the bars and talk to people about the Lord. He would be on drugs and yet he talked about the Lord so much. He truly was fighting a spiritual battle. Paul and his girlfriend started going to Church with me. He would be messed up on drugs and was so faithful at church. My son would read the bible so much. It was as though he was starving for God's word. I asked God one day "why isn't Paul doing what's right?" God, he is reading your word everyday. Why is he still drinking? God so plainly told me. He knows my words, but he has not given me his heart. Satan knows God's words. When you come to God you have to give him your heart. It is a heartfelt relationship between you and the Lord. The most intelligent person in the world could be so lost. It is not about how intelligent you are. Matthew 22 verses 37-39 Thou shalt love the Lord they God with all thy heart, and with all thy soul, and with all thy mind. This is the first and great commandment. And the second is like unto it, Thou shalt love thy neighbor as thyself. Romans chapter 1 verse 22: Professing themselves to be wise, they became fools.

My husband was not handling it well at all. When my husband would see our son all he would do is cruse him and call him all kinds of names. That was the way my husband would handle it. He said "I have to get away for awhile." My husband did not have the Lord helping him through this like I did.

About a month before that we told our son to leave and that he could not stay in the trailer next to us. We pretty much kicked him out. That was a hard thing to do. I went over to see my son one day and see where he was living. I took him some things he could use. It truly broke my heart. He lived in a trailer house with all the windows broken out and there was no carpet or tile on the floors. It was in the hot part of the summer. It would be in the 100's during the day. He had no air conditioner, stove or icebox. Just a bed, ice chest and a box fan. My son lived right behind the bar where his girlfriend Connie worked. I asked my son to go outside and sit in the car with me. I started talking to him about getting his life together. All of a sudden I started prophesying to Paul. That was my first time to do that. Paul was telling me he had to help straighten the world up. God told him "that the battle belongs to me. This is not your fight. To walk the narrow path to God and let God handle this. Stop hurting yourself and your parents." I sat there for about an hour talking to my son. Then I left and went home so broken hearted about where he lived and that he was so lost. I told my husband and he said "you have to let him go and that is all we can do." I must have handed him over to God so many times, but I never let him go. I was still hanging on with all my might. We say we hand things over to God when we really don't.

My husband wanted to get away for the weekend. I wanted to help my son so much. That weekend came when Don went to a cabin at the lake. We needed time apart as well. Our relationship was not going well. I came in from work that day and started thinking about my son. That was all I did. I could not get Paul off my mind. I called the bar where his girlfriend Connie worked. I asked her if they had plans that night and she said "no." I said "would you both like a cool place to lay your heads tonight and sleep where it is cool? I will cook you both dinner and you can wash some clothes. She said "we would love too."

I was excited they were coming to the house. I started cooking dinner and couldn't wait for them to get there. When they got there she started washing clothes and they both ate supper. I fixed Paul's favorite dish. Then we talked for awhile and I went to bed. I heard their truck start up and I got up to see what was going on. I went outside and Connie said they were fighting and that Paul had left. I was

Dreams and Visions ~

upset that he left. I was trying my best to help him. I went back to bed and he came back before long. I just stayed in bed and left them alone.

The next morning they left early because she had to go to work at the bar. They were attending church and went to almost every service. I felt like it didn't help at all by inviting them to the house. I thought I have done all I can. About an hour after they left the house the phone rang. I answered it and it was my son Paul. He said "mom I am coming off a high on drugs and I want help. Get me some help mom. I will go to a rehab place." I told him to come back to the house and I will make some phone calls and get him some help. Before he got there I was on the phone trying to get him some help. It took most of the day. I called a friend of mine Mary to come over and help me to get him some help. We found a place where he could go. Paul had to get a court order from a judge to get into the rehab. He got the court order and was in rehab in just a couple of days. The rehab was not ran the way it should have been. That place was just out to make money and did not care about helping them. It was not where Paul should be. He only stayed about one week.

Then he came home. It has been about six months and Paul has not taken drugs. I thank God so much that he got off the drugs. I guess if you truly want to stop drugs you can. It was very hard to see him live in that old torn-up trailer in the hottest part of summer. I now know it was the right thing to do. Now he needs help with his drinking. My son now realizes that he had no friends. They were all using him. Even his best friend Randy was using him. The one true friend you can count on is Jesus. He is there all the time and will never leave you.

You can only take so much in life. My marriage was not going well. I have been going to church about nineteen years without my husband. We were growing apart so much. He just got angry and shouts and cures at me or my son all the time. It was like he had to be mad all the time. He was either mad at me or our son. We needed each other through what we were going through with our son. We didn't agree on things. I had God and he had anger and his beer. My husband would tell my son not to drink and standing there with a beer in his hand.

I worked four days a week and had our granddaughter three days a week. I had no time to myself. I told my husband that I love our granddaughter, but that I need time for myself. My husband would not listen to me. He said "you should be ashamed of yourself. I could keep the baby all the time." My husband was disabled and did not work. He was home all the time. I told him several times that I needed time for myself. My doctor told me I needed time for myself. I had to get on blood pressure pills and anti-depressions pills, because of all the stress. I took anti-depression pills for about four months. I wanted off them so I asked my doctor and she said ok.

My husband and I would disagree so much about things. He would get mad and tell me if I didn't like it around here to go get a divorce. This house is mine house and I am not leaving. He told me that a lot of times. He told me that I needed to get back on anti-depression pills. One day we had the baby and we were disagreeing on things. I was still telling him I needed time for myself and he got mad. I went to walk outside and I heard him tell our granddaughter that is two and a half years old that her meme didn't love her anymore and that she did not want her. Those words went all through me. It was on a Sunday morning.

~ Linda Wells

I got ready for church and got the baby ready too. I walked over to my son's house and told him what had happened. I could not believe that my husband said that. I was furious. I went to church that day. When we came home from church I told my son, "take the baby and I will be back in a little while." So I went to my friend Mary's house and talked to her. I went back home and I thought about all the things I went through in my marriage. Never before could I walk out and leave. It was as though God took me by the hand and lead me out the door that day. I truly believe I could not have left a day earlier or a day later. I left with God holding my hand. I got some clothes and stayed with my son for a week. I found out that he was still drinking and we had words. My son would treat me as bad as his dad did, when he would drink and get upset. I told my son I am not putting up with the way your dad treats me. I am not going to put up with you doing the same thing. I packed my clothes and left. I didn't know where I was going, but I had enough. All I wanted to do is get away from the drinking and cursing. I wanted to find some peace that I had longed for a long time. I

Dreams and Visions ~

thought of my friend Janet and went to her house and she said I could stay as long as I wanted.

Within one week I found a small apartment. This is where I am now. God has told me to finish this book. I now have the peace to write this book. God truly gave me such peace when I left. The peace I felt is indescribable. I was driving down the road one day and I was asking God "Is this the right thing to do? Is it ok for me to leave a marriage of thirty-three years?" I wanted the Lord to tell me it was ok. I heard a voice telling me that I never intended for your life to be this way. I am going to open doors for you and you will be fine. You have always put your husband and son first. It is your time to be first. Matthew chapter 7 verse 7 and 8: Ask, and it shall be given you; seek, and ye shall find; knock, and it shall be opened unto you: For every one that asketh receiveth; and he that seeketh findeth; and to him that knocketh it shall be opened.

Never before could I walk out and be on my own. I stepped out on faith. Within two weeks after I left my husband, I went and filed for a divorce. I know that I have done all I can for my husband and son. I have truly left them in God's hands this time. I know that my husband and son are getting closer by my leaving. My son is very hurt that I left. I did not hear from my son for about two weeks. He was not going to church. I thought he might have quit. One day he called me and asked how I was doing. I told him I was doing ok. Paul told me he had been sick with the flu. He said that is why he was not in church. We talked for awhile on the phone. I asked him if he would like to meet me the next day and visit. He said ok and I had a great visit with my son. I know he will be ok. God has protected him through all of this.

Paul went to court on his DUI and they want him to go to rehab. I truly don't know what it will take for him to stop the drinking. Sometimes when we truly love them, we just have to let go. God can and will do what is best for him. It is not easy, but I know God has control over all things. There is times when we have to walk alone, so God can lead us to where he wants us to be. I know God has a place for Paul to serve and do God's work. God has watched over him so much. I have to remember what it took for me to come to the Lord. It was watching a man take his last breath. I pray that he realizes there are so many good things in life. His daughter is the most precious thing. I want him to be a good dad and cherish the time he can have with her. As each day goes by he is missing out on time with his daughter.

Life is too short to live in such an unhappy place. I know with all my heart there is a better life. I don't know what is ahead for me. I know the Lord will make a way for me. Sometime we just have to have faith and step out and follow the Lord. It is up to us to how close of a relationship we have with the Lord. The Lord is always there. How many steps are you taking to the Lord? I find myself taking more and more steps to the Lord. We will always grow in the Lord each and every day. I have prayed for strength, peace and wisdom from the Lord. The Lord is filling my cup until it is running over. Thank you Jesus for all you have given me. You have given me so many gifts.

We never know how people feel as they are going through bad times in life. We can just image and that is it. Until we have walk in the same area of life they have. I have been blessed with my friends around and helping me. My friends have blessed me more than they know. If we have the Lord in our life and lean on him, we will survive in this world. Just knowing someday I will be in heaven with my Lord keeps me going here in this old world. I am not of this world. I am just passing through it.

We will always have things to go through in life, but the Lord is there to help us get through them. The Lord gives me the strength I need when I need it. I am so thankful that I can talk to the Lord anytime about anything. Sometimes I feel that is the only one I can truly talk too about some things. I am still going to church by myself. I will always pray for my son and Don. I wish the best for both of them. I will never give up on them. God never gave up on me. It is that I have to go on with my life. We will go through hardships and trails, but there is revelation.

It does not cost us anything to be saved. For Jesus paid the price. We are sinners saved by God's grace. It is as easy as A B C: A- admit that you are a sinner. B-believe that Jesus died on the cross for your sins. C- confess your sins to Jesus. We are not perfect and never will be. The love Jesus has for us he showed upon the cross. Acts 2 verse 21. And it shall come to pass, that whosoever shall call upon the name of the Lord shall be saved.

It was not my choice to write this book. The Lord chose me to write this book. I started feeling so uncomfortable. I keep thinking about the book. I said "Lord I can't write a book." I kept thinking about it and could not get it off my mind. One night in my sleep I saw the book cover so plainly. I knew then I was going to write this book. I said "Lord I know you will be guiding me all the way." So give God the glory for this book and all he has done in your life.

What Things Has God Done for You?

What Have You Done to Serve Others?

If You Had One Prayer, What Would it Be?

CPSIA information can be obtained at www.ICGtesting.com
Printed in the USA
LVOW13s1807240813

349379LV00001B/3/P